Christopher Columbus

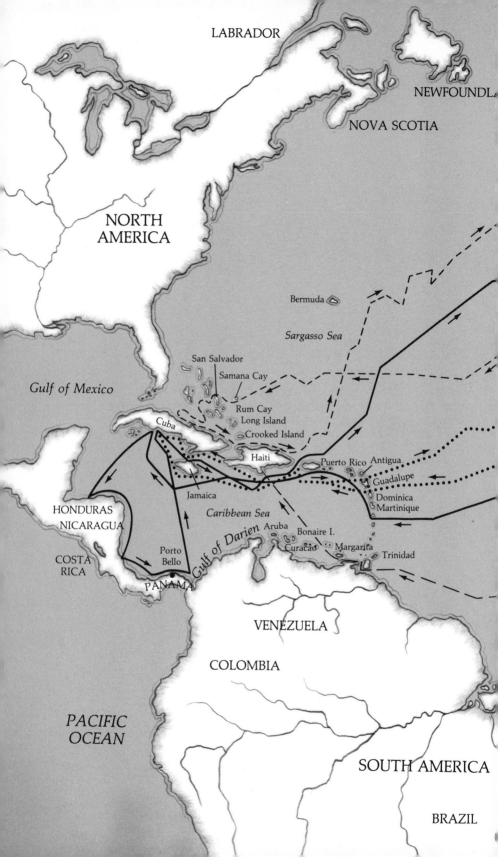

LABRADOR

NEWFOUNDLA[ND]

NOVA SCOTIA

NORTH
AMERICA

Bermuda

Sargasso Sea

Gulf of Mexico

San Salvador
Samana Cay
Rum Cay
Long Island
Cuba
Crooked Island
Haiti
Puerto Rico   Antigua
Guadalupe
Jamaica
Dominica
Martinique
HONDURAS
NICARAGUA
Caribbean Sea
COSTA
RICA
Porto
Bello
Aruba   Bonaire I.
Curaçao   Margarita
Gulf of Darien   Trinidad
PANAMA

VENEZUELA

COLOMBIA

PACIFIC
OCEAN

SOUTH AMERICA

BRAZIL

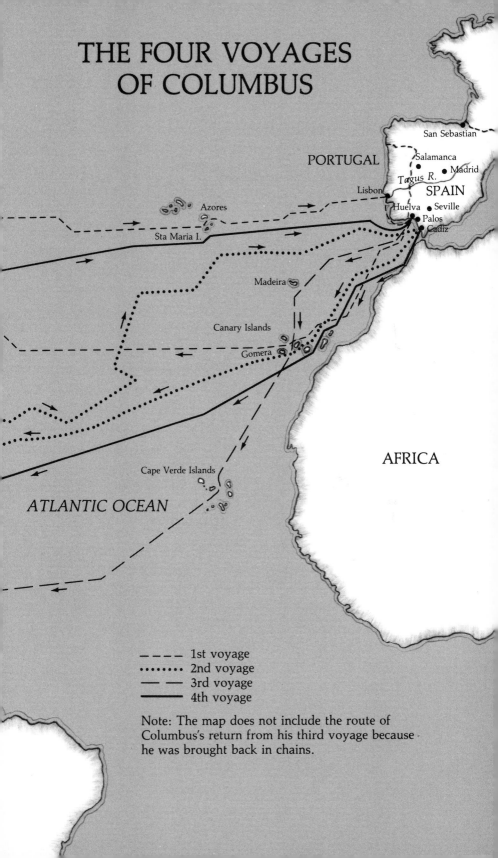

THE FOUR VOYAGES
OF COLUMBUS

San Sebastian

PORTUGAL

Salamanca

Madrid

Tagus R.

SPAIN

Lisbon

Huelva · Seville

Azores

Palos

Cadiz

Sta Maria I.

Madeira

Canary Islands

Gomera

AFRICA

Cape Verde Islands

ATLANTIC OCEAN

– – – – 1st voyage
· · · · · · · 2nd voyage
— — — 3rd voyage
——— 4th voyage

Note: The map does not include the route of
Columbus's return from his third voyage because
he was brought back in chains.

CHRISTOPHER COLUMBUS

on the Green Sea of Darkness

GARDNER SOULE

Franklin Watts   New York   London   Toronto   Sydney   1988

Library of Congress Cataloging-in-Publication Data

Soule, Gardner.
Christopher Columbus: on the green sea of darkness/Gardner Soule.
p.   cm.
Bibliography: p.
Includes index.
Summary: Describes the voyages of Christopher Columbus, detailing
the events and discoveries connected with each.
ISBN 0-531-10577-6
1. Columbus, Christopher—Juvenile literature. 2. Explorers—
America—Biography—Juvenile literature. 3. Explorers—Spain—
Biography—Juvenile literature. 4. America—Discovery and
exploration—Spanish—Juvenile literature. [1. America—Discovery
and exploration—Spanish. 2. Columbus, Christopher. 3. Explorers.]
I. Title.
E111.S7 1988
970.01′5—dc19
[92]   88-14262 CIP AC

Dedicated to

Marjory Rogers Kline
Maury Solomon
Lydia Stein
Jennie Parrish Rakos

Contents

Christopher Columbus

Chapter One

THREE LIGHTS
IN THE NIGHT,
FAR AT SEA

There were, after dark, three small, lonesome gleams of light—far from shore. They bobbed with the waves.

No other lights were to be seen. None at all—none north, south, east, or west. Each of the lights was a lantern—a lantern hung at the stern of a small wooden sailing ship. The lights were the only way the ships had to keep in touch with each other.

There were no other vessels on the Atlantic where they were traveling. Only a few ships and a few people in all history before them had attempted to sail this trackless sea. Of those before them, most had not returned—had never been heard from again.

At the time, 1492, when the three ships had ventured onto the Atlantic, that ocean was feared and dreaded. This was largely due to the influence of an important group of Mediterranean people, the Muslims (Moslems or Mohammedans). The Muslims controlled North Africa—as they do today—all the way to the Atlantic. They had even governed Spain until 1492. Previously, the Muslims had occupied and influenced Portugal as well.

The Muslims, including the Moors, or Arabs of northwest Africa, avoided the Atlantic Ocean. Although the Moors were at the time excellent sailors and navigators in the Red Sea, and on the Indian Ocean on the other side of Africa, they feared the Atlantic and referred to it as the Green Sea of Darkness or the Green Sea of Night.

Whirlpools, an Arab said—it could have been their great traveler, Ibn Battuta (1304?–1378?)—destroyed anyone who ventured onto the Atlantic.

The Muslims, in fact, had such a horror of the western ocean, the Atlantic, that they believed a sailor who dared this unknown sea was not sane and so should not be allowed normal citizenship.

The officers and crews of the three lonesome ships carrying the lanterns knew all this perfectly well. They also knew that a few ships had come home from unknown seas, and that vessels that did return might bring home valuable information—about new lands, new fishing grounds, new countries to trade with. A trip across an almost-unknown ocean might be worthwhile.

No one could know it, those first nights out, but this trip would be. The three specks of light on the ocean marked the start of a voyage that would change the world.

In Columbus's day, the Muslims dreaded
the Atlantic Ocean and called it the
Green Sea of Darkness, or the Green Sea
of Night. Monsters were believed to be
in the ocean. The one at left turned out
to be real: the ten-armed giant squid.
It weighed up to two tons; its longest
tentacles were up to 50 feet.

The lights first burned on the night of September 9, 1492. The man who ordered them lit, the commander of the three ships, was Christopher Columbus.

Chapter Two

THE SEA CALLS

Columbus was born sometime between August 25 and October 31, 1451. His father, Domenico Colombo, was a wool weaver, a respected citizen of Genoa, Italy. His mother's maiden name was Susanna Fontanarossa. The name of Domenico and Susanna's firstborn in Portuguese or Spanish was Cristóbal Colón, in Italian, Cristoforo Colombo, in English—Christopher Columbus. Christopher had a brother about a year younger, Bartholomew; a sister, Bianchetta; a brother who died young; and another brother seventeen years younger than Christopher, Diego or Giacomo.

Genoa, a sunny seaport of Liguria, was full of fishing boats and big and little freight ships, and was a town where charts and maps were made and sold.

From early childhood, Columbus would have heard sailors' tales of voyaging to unknown or almost-unknown seas. The lad would have gazed at the ships coming and going. He would have talked to sailors, merchants, boatbuilders, mapmakers. He would have heard lore of the eastern Mediterranean Sea—the center of the ancient world—where Egyptians, Phoenicians, Cretans, Cypriots, Greeks, and Romans had sailed. Here some of their sailors must have been among the first to go out of sight of land, to sail (by the sun and the north star) beyond the horizon, on into unknown seas.

From Italy itself, the Romans under Julius Caesar had sailed beyond the Mediterranean out into the Atlantic and all the way to Britain (then unknown to the Romans). In A.D. 42 they had sailed around Britain and learned it was an island.

The Romans had called the Atlantic the Dark Sea. The name may have turned into the Muslims' Green Sea of Darkness.

At sea, out of Genoa, the teenage Columbus went on at least two trips to the Greek island of Chios. He was on Homer's and Ulysses' wine-dark sea, where so many mariners had sailed, and from where they—especially the Phoenicians and Greeks—had gone on beyond countless horizons to cross and crisscross the Mediterranean.

In 1476, as a seaman from Genoa bound for Lisbon, Portugal, Columbus was aboard a ship that was attacked and sunk off Cape St. Vincent, Portugal, one of Europe's most westerly points in the Atlantic, named for a Christian martyr. To the saint, in Columbus's time, Christian ships dipped their sails as they passed.

Columbus, wounded, was dumped into the sea and clung to an oar to keep afloat. He somehow managed to paddle six miles (9.6 km) to shore. Then he went on to Lisbon.

For most of the 1400s, just before Columbus, Cape St. Vincent had been the base of Prince Henry of Portugal. Here Henry had maintained what he called a naval school. He had hired ships' captains, shipbuilders, mapmakers, astronomers, mathematicians, instrument-makers, and anyone else who might help to improve ships and sailing.

From 1415 to 1460, Henry sent one captain after another south down the then-unknown, unexplored, and unreached Atlantic coast of Africa. South his captains went—each year a hundred miles (160 km) more, if possible, into unknown seas.

The purpose: to try to find a way around Africa and to sail on east to Asia, to India, to bring back spices. Spices were a major need of Europeans. Spices made stale food eatable. And in the 1400s there was no refrigeration, no canning, no preserving in glass jars—and lots of stale and spoiled food.

After Prince Henry's death, in 1460, Portuguese ships continued to go south along the African coast.

But at the time Columbus reached Lisbon, no vessel had ever sailed all the way to the southern tip of Africa. Sailors wondered if there *was* a southern end to Africa, if there was a way around it.

When Columbus arrived in Lisbon in the 1470s he was in his twenties, tall, muscular, red-haired, gray- or blue-eyed, and freckled. He had come to join his brother Bartholomew, who had lived there for some time, making charts and maps and selling them to ships' officers and captains.

Lisbon was a good place to sell charts and maps—and a good place for a sailor to look for a job. Not only was it a center of shipping for Europe, it was in fact the principal and busiest port at the time. From Lisbon, ships sailed east to the far end of the Mediterranean Sea; north to France, Britain, Ireland, and Germany; and south down the African coast. On the Lisbon waterfront, Columbus would have heard about the voyages of Prince Henry's sailors. Every year he would have heard of one trip or more south down the coast of Africa: beyond the known world of Europeans, around the bulge of Africa, on to the island of Fernando Po (now called Bioko), across the equator—a milestone because people had wondered if they could survive tropical heat or would be broiled alive.

Christopher Columbus
—one representation.
No two of the supposed
pictures of Columbus
appear similar.

DETECTOR ✝ CHRISTOPHORVS COLVMBVS GENVENSIS PRIMVS NOVARVM TERRARVM

NOVA DVM BONA
P
C

Columbus did get work in Lisbon. On at least one occasion he is believed to have made a trip south down the African coast to a settlement founded by Prince Henry's people.

But no ship from Europe in the 1470s had reached all the way to the southernmost tip of Africa, today's Cape Agulhas, near the Cape of Good Hope.

Chapter Three

A SEASONED
SAILOR

In the later part of 1476, having attained another berth as a sailor, Columbus sailed to Flanders (Belgium), Germany, Great Britain, and western Ireland.

In Ireland, Columbus might have heard of another voyager to unknown seas: Brendan, an Irish monk. In A.D. 565–573, Brendan traveled, or was supposed to have traveled, to unknown places in the Atlantic Ocean.

Brendan's tale was told all over Europe by wandering minstrels. The story became a romance to generations of drudging Europeans—a tale of escape to a happier, Utopian island.

In time, Brendan was made a saint. His tale, once believed to be fictitious, may be all or largely true.

In 1477, Columbus, still a young seaman, reached a sea unknown to him—and strange to most Europe-

Before Columbus, an Irish monk, later
St. Brendan, went to sea in an open boat,
landed on a whale, and found, to the west,
a merman, whales, and unknown islands.
The story, told by minstrels, intrigued
sailors and people all over Europe.

ans: the Arctic Ocean north of Iceland. Columbus would have been twenty-six years old.

In a later letter to his son Fernando, Columbus wrote:

> *I sailed in the year 1477, in the month of February, a hundred leagues beyond Thule [that is, Iceland] . . . to this island . . . the Englishmen go with merchandise . . . at the time I went there, the sea was frozen even though there were huge tides. . . .*

The idea of Columbus, the young man from the warm Mediterranean, on a trip to the Arctic is surprising.

In Iceland, Columbus could have heard about the Vikings' or Norsemen's voyages across the then-unknown Atlantic to lands they had reached farther west: Greenland and Vinland (North America). One Viking, Bjarni Harjolfsson, had glimpsed Vinland in the late tenth century A.D. Leif Ericsson almost certainly landed in Vinland around 1000.

In 1478, Columbus sailed from Lisbon to Porto Santo, a 7-mile-long (11-km) island in the Madeira Islands, and then on to Genoa.

The daughter of the first governor of Porto Santo in the Madeiras was to become Columbus's bride. She was Felipa Moniz de Perestrello (or Palestrello). Both her father and her grandfather had been Portuguese navigators.

The year after the wedding Felipa gave birth to Columbus's first son, Diego.

Partly through the Perestrello family, partly through his brother Bartholomew and the chart-selling business, and partly because of his own experiences as a sailor, Columbus became well acquainted with Portuguese sailors and captains.

In Porto Santo, visiting his wife's family, Columbus must have met mariners who believed in exploring or crossing the Atlantic westward. By sailing south, and west, in the Atlantic, they had found islands—the Madeiras and the Canaries and the Cape Verdes and the Azores.

At Porto Santo, Columbus would have heard that the ocean to the west was full of mysteries. He would have heard of the bodies of strange men (American Indians?) sometimes washed ashore on some of the islands. He could have heard tales of strange logs (driftwood from trees not grown in Europe) or of strange plants sometimes washed ashore. The sea bean, for example, the seed of a Caribbean Islands' woody climber, floats on the ocean because it contains an air space inside it and is often washed up in the Azores and at Madeira.

Columbus would have heard from many sailors that they had gazed westward and seen islands or an unknown coast. Many sailors scanning the wide ocean in those days thought they had seen such things.

One sailor the red-headed Columbus certainly met in Porto Santo was his wife's brother-in-law, Pedro Correo. Correo is said to have told Columbus of seeing carved wood—but not carved with iron—

that had drifted to Porto Santo. Europeans, of course, carved with iron; someone unknown must have carved the driftwood.

And in Porto Santo, Columbus could—almost certainly would—have pored over the charts of his late father-in-law, Bartholomew Perestrello, the navigator.

In 1479, Columbus traveled to Prince Henry's African coast to help build a fort called St. George at El Mina on the Gold Coast. Back in Lisbon in 1482, he was acknowledged a first-class pilot and navigator.

Chapter Four

A TURNING POINT
IN HISTORY

From 1482 to 1484, Columbus was in the service of Portugal. Some time before 1484, Columbus, who was then around thirty-two years old—middle age in the 1400s—submitted to the king of Portugal, John, a plan to seek Asia and spices by sailing west.

Columbus, in proposing to sail west to Asia, believed, as did others of his day, that the globe was considerably smaller than it actually is. A short trip across the Atlantic to Asia was considered a possibility. Columbus did not know—nobody knew—that North America and Central America and South America and the Pacific Ocean were in the way.

The king in 1484 had plenty of experienced sailors on his payroll, and, because he did, he felt he did not need Columbus for this task.

He rejected Columbus's plan.

As if the king's rejection were not enough, in 1485 Columbus's wife, Felipa, died. This left him with a five-year-old son, Diego, to raise.

Columbus went to Spain where he sought to gain an audience with the gifted and pious Queen Isabella, who, with her consort, King Ferdinand, ruled over the kingdoms of Castile and Aragon. Perhaps she would finance his expedition. Meanwhile, to obtain food, lodging, and an education for Diego, he placed the boy at a monastery, La Rábida, near Palos.

In 1487, for the king of Portugal, Bartholomew Diaz (Bartolomeo Dias) went south down Africa's Atlantic Ocean coast. He reached frigid seas, was out of sight of land for thirteen days, and barely rounded the tip of Africa. That was enough.

That was enough to show that there probably would be a way east to Asia—and spices—around Africa.

Diaz had made a great discovery.

Diaz named the cape at the southern tip of Africa the Cape of Storms. Because it offered hope of a route to Asia, King John of Portugal changed the name to the Cape of Good Hope.

On March 20, 1488, King John wrote to Columbus asking him to return to Portugal. Columbus did.

Nothing came of it except that Columbus was able to witness Diaz's return: "He described his trip and recorded it on a nautical chart, league by league, in order to be able to present this to the eyes of the king. I was present when this happened."

Brother Bartholomew Columbus, meanwhile, set out in 1488 to win support from Henry VII of England

ARCTIC OCEAN

GREENLAND

Baffen Bay

ICELAND

Labrador

NORTH AMERICA

ASIA

EUROPE

SPAIN

PORTUGAL

Azores

Lisbon

Porto Santo

Madeira Is.

Sanlúcar

Palos

Canary Is.

ATLANTIC OCEAN

ARABIA

INDI

Cape Verde Is.

AFRICA

INDIAN OCEAN

SOUTH AMERICA

Cape of Good Hope

PRINCIPAL VOYAGES OF DISCOVERY BEFORE 1492

—————— Bjarni Harjolfsson 986

– – – – – Leif Ericsson 1001

—·—·— Bartholomew Diaz 1487–1488

or from Charles VIII of France for a voyage west by Christopher. Bartholomew was shipwrecked and never got the assistance.

Also in 1488, Columbus's second son, Fernando (Ferdinand), was born. His mother was Beatriz Enriquez de Harana.

Columbus, back in Spain, again sought backing from Queen Isabella. The same age as Columbus, the auburn-haired, blue-eyed queen was charmed by Columbus; they were to be lifelong friends. Yet Columbus, asking aid so he could sail west across the Atlantic Ocean, was time and again rejected.

But a date that would be significant in history was to help Columbus. For seven hundred years Spain had been occupied and ruled by the Moors. On January 2, 1492, Ferdinand and Isabella fought—and won—the last battle against them. The last great Moorish stronghold in Spain, Granada, surrendered.

The Reconquista—the Reconquest—had been achieved, one of the milestones of Spain's history. With his own eyes, Columbus saw the wild, joyous celebration of Spain's victory. The country was independent; Spain at long last could think about other things.

Still, Columbus did not sell his idea at once. For the past ten years, he had tried—and failed—to get assistance: from Portugal, England, France, and, repeatedly, from Spain. Disillusioned, despairing, he left the court of Ferdinand and Isabella.

*King Ferdinand and Queen Isabella,
in 1492, drove the Muslims out of
Spain and later supported Columbus.*

Sometimes riding a mule, sometimes plodding along the sandy land, Columbus reached a point near Huelva, a little maritime town near Cadiz. Here he was sent for and asked to return to the Spanish court. Columbus did, but failing again to come to terms, once more he departed, this time headed for France.

That same day—in February 1492—a messenger on horseback was sent after him, and overtook him at a bridge in the village of Pinos-Puente, 10 miles (16 km) from Granada.

Encountering a discouraged, dusty, utterly tired Columbus, the messenger told him that the queen had decided to back his venture. The moment was a turning point in history.

Columbus turned his mule around. For what must have seemed to him the umpteenth time, he returned to the Spanish court.

This time he got his help.

Chapter Five

THE BEST SHIPS—WITH PROBLEMS

The help given Columbus by Queen Isabella and King Ferdinand took the form of three ships—the *Niña*, the *Pinta*, and the *Santa María*—that on August 3, 1492, under the command of Columbus, moved out of the port of Palos in southwest Spain. They would travel, Columbus had said, by a route "by which down to this day we do not know certainly that anyone has passed."

The largest of Columbus's three vessels, the *Santa María*, perhaps 90 feet (27 m) long, was owned by a man who was along, Juan de la Cosa. The *Santa María* carried a crew of about forty men. Her sails may have been of a blue cotton cloth—denim or serge de Nîmes—from a textile town in southern France.

The *Pinta*, 56 feet (17 m) or longer, with about twenty-six men, had as captain a man who was both an experienced sailor and a substantial citizen of Pa-

Columbus's three ships carried a cross on square
sails. Atop the mast flew the banner of Ferdinand
and Isabella. The Niña started with lateen (fore-
and-aft) sails as at right, but when she reached
the Canary Islands changed to square sails.

los, Martin Alonso Pinzón. His brother, Francisco Pinzón, was the ship's pilot.

The *Niña*, with eighteen to twenty-four men, 67 or 70 feet (20 or 21 m) long, had as captain a third brother, Vicente Yáñez Pinzón. The *Niña* had a beam of about 21 or 23 feet (6 or 7 m), and a draft of only 6 or 7 feet (1.8 or 2 m). *Niña* in Spanish means "girl" or "little girl."

We have no plans of Columbus's vessels. The *Santa María* may have been a caravel. She may have been a nao. Authorities disagree. A nao was a ship with a high bow and stern, a crow's nest for a lookout at the masthead, and a fixed rudder at the stern.

The *Niña* and the *Pinta* are generally believed to have been caravels. A caravel could use triangular fore-and-aft (lateen) sails, and therefore could better sail into the wind. A caravel could also use square sails, rigged across the width of the ship, to run before the wind. To cross the Atlantic, Columbus would use square sails.

A caravel had, instead of the old single mast of a sailing ship, two or three or even four masts. The *Niña* had four.* A caravel had a high bow and stern. There was a fixed rudder at the stern. Ranging in

*For years, Columbus's ship *Niña* was thought to have two or three masts. Not long ago historian Eugene Lyon turned up a fifteenth-century document showing the *Niña* with four masts. The document, the *Libro de Armadas*, is a 400-page description of caravel fleets to the New World, 1455–1500. (National Geographic Society, news release October 8, 1986.)

Columbus's favorite ship was the Niña *(Girl or* Little Girl*). According to a fifteenth-century record found by historian Eugene Lyon, she had four masts. She used square sails to cross the Atlantic.*

length from 35 feet (10.6 m) (the length of two automobiles) to 70 feet (21 m), or even longer, caravels were light, shallow in draft (as was the *Niña* with her need for only 6 or 7 feet (1.8 or 2 m) of water beneath her), easier to manage than earlier ships, and fairly easily kept off rocks and shoals.

A caravel in 1492 was the latest thing in transportation.

Columbus's ships, the best of their day, had the faults of ships of their time as well. This meant that Columbus's crews dared the Green Sea of Darkness with all sorts of difficulties.

The vessels were leaky. To keep out seawater, the men had only wooden pumps that they worked at till their backs, legs, shoulders, and arms ached. The caravels were hard to sail and hard to steer. They had no plumbing. They had bad odors. They were filthy. There were lice, cockroaches, rats.

Some of the things Columbus's ships did not have would leave a modern sailor aghast. They had no electricity. They had no wireless, or radio: no way to communicate with the shore, no way to call for help, no way to communicate with each other except by those lanterns or by drawing close together and shouting—not easy in rough weather.

They had no such things as navigation satellites.

They had no clocks—no accurate way to keep time—only sandglasses. Every thirty minutes, when the sand in the top of the glass had run to the bottom, the cabin boy, if he had been able to keep himself awake, turned over the sandglass.

These sailors on the Green Sea of Darkness had no sonar, no echo-sounding, to measure the depths beneath them. They had no radar to show obstacles—another ship, a shoreline—through a fog. They had no barometers to warn of impending or approaching storms. They had no telescopes. None. Telescopes would not be invented for another hundred years.

They did have compasses, such as they were, in the late 1400s. They had the astrolabe and the quadrant to determine their approximate position from stars or sun.

Ashore or afloat, in 1492, there was no refrigeration of any kind to keep food fresh. To make matters worse, there was no canning and there was no preserving food in glass jars. Bread and biscuits soon became wormy. Salted beef or pork soon rotted—especially in warm climates. Wine and water spoiled in their casks.

The cook had only a small, open firebox that might provide one hot meal a day. In rough weather, when he could not keep the fire lit, there were no hot meals at all.

Seasickness, a miserable condition, often affected everyone aboard.

To get the ships underway, some of the crews had to man heavy oars, or sweeps. To do so was to use muscles as they did on the pumps: till the muscles ached.

In spite of all their shortcomings, the caravels were still the best long-distance transportation people had ever had. Said a navigator from Venice, Alvise de Cadamosto (who had worked for Portugal's Prince Henry): "I see no reason why these caravels should not sail anywhere in the sea." With Columbus, and with many sailors after him, they would sail for another hundred years.

Chapter Six

ONTO AN
ALMOST UNKNOWN
OCEAN

In August and September 1492, Columbus, forty or forty-one years old, and his captains and crews, made a stop at the Canary Islands. From the Canaries, the islanders had sworn for years that they sometimes glimpsed land far away to the west.

Columbus's sailors were not cheered up when they saw what was, to sailors of their day, "a bad omen": a volcano on the Canary island of Tenerife erupted.

They went ahead anyway.

On this trip, Columbus wrote down each day what happened and what he saw. He was one of the first sailors to keep a log, or journal.

On September 6, 1492, Columbus and his people turned their backs on the Canary Islands and headed west: due west—west out of sight of land—west beyond the horizon—west across the Green Sea of Darkness.

With their less-than-perfect compasses, they sought to follow the latitude of the Canaries: about 28 degrees north of the equator. The Canaries were thought to be on the same latitude as Cipangu, or Japan, and so, they reasoned, by sailing due west, they would reach Cipangu, never before visited by a European.

Pushing the three little ships westward were the northeast trade winds—strong, often steady winds that Prince Henry's earlier Portuguese sailors had experienced in the Canaries. Also helpful was a current that flows toward the west, the north equatorial current, or drift.

They saw another bad omen soon after they left the Canaries: "a large piece of the mast" of a sunken ship, Columbus wrote in his journal, floated past.

They sailed on.

By the night of September 9, 1492, the Canary Islands had vanished entirely below the horizon, and the ninety men and boys in their three small ships were alone on an uncharted sea.

Every night thereafter, the single lantern at each ship's stern would keep the vessels together.

Chapter Seven

BEYOND
THE HORIZON

September 13, 1492. Columbus noticed the movement west of the north equatorial drift, and made one of the first written records of an observation of a current by any sailor, anywhere.

All the time, Columbus noted in his journal, he had temperate breezes and lovely mornings.

On September 14–15, the sailors were frightened: they saw a meteor. Said Columbus: "And on this night, at the beginning of it, they saw fall from the sky a marvelous branch of fire."

On September 16, and for several days thereafter, the three ships sailed through what has become known as the Sargasso Sea. The Sargasso is 2 million square miles (5 million sq km) of water in the blue mid-Atlantic; it surrounds Bermuda.

It is the sea inside a system of currents that, we know today, moves slowly and unceasingly around the North Atlantic, in the same direction as a clock's hands move. Although the currents, including the Gulf Stream and the north equatorial drift, sometimes shift their positions, they always move at 2 or 3 knots around the Sargasso Sea. That would be about a person's walking speed, a little over 2 or 3 miles (3 or 5 km) an hour.

From one or more old-time Portuguese sailors, Columbus had heard of the Sargasso Sea. He had heard that it has vast amounts of floating seaweed. The Portuguese called the weed *sargasso;* we call it sargassum weed. It is a plant, a brown alga, that is enabled to float by small grape-shaped, air-filled bladders.

Upon the weed in midocean there live many animals. They include an insect, *Halobates*—the water strider—which breathes air and therefore would drown if it fell off into the sea. It is the only insect (though there are a number of species of it) in all the oceans of the world. *Halobates* is the sea-going member of the insect family Gerridae, the pond skaters, or water striders.

On September 17, Columbus's men picked up some of the weed and found on it a green, thumb-nail-size crab.

One day the whole ocean was covered with green and yellow weed.

Columbus lowered a weighted line overboard to measure the depth of the Sargasso Sea. At one point he let out 200 fathoms, or 1200 feet (360 m) (the entire length of his line), but failed to reach the bottom—where today we have measured the Atlantic at 2450 fathoms deep.

On September 18, the men saw many birds and a ridge of low clouds that suggested land. Sailors of the time constantly watched birds. The flights of birds had helped lead the Portuguese to the Canary and Cape Verde islands, and hawks, we think, had led the Portuguese to the Azores.

Some of the birds seen by Columbus and his crews almost certainly were storm petrels—Mother Carey's chickens—that feed in midocean, and most of the time live there, flitting just above the waves.

The sailors kept hoping the birds indicated that land was nearby. Storm petrels would not necessarily mean that; they stay for months far at sea.

On September 20, the men saw boobies (West Indies gannet) and other birds; again land was believed near. Columbus again sounded to 200 fathoms—and again found no bottom.

With fishing lines overboard, the crew caught dorados, the green-blue-and-silver dolphin fish which can grow up to 6 feet (1.8 m) long. As one died on the deck, its colors faded fast. (The fish is not the same as the mammal known as the dolphin or porpoise.)

The men saw flying fish as well.

On September 25, said Columbus in his journal, "The sea was very smooth so that many sailors went swimming."

Columbus in mid-ocean may have seen storm petrels,
5-inch-long birds that spend their lives far
at sea. Sailors in Columbus's day followed birds
to land, but storm petrels, staying at sea,
would not have been useful guides.

That same day, Martin Alonso Pinzón, captain of the *Pinta,* shouted, "Land! Land!" It was, said a later biographer of Columbus, "a towering cumulus cloud, common enough in trade-wind latitudes," but not common to Columbus's sailors. Next day, Columbus called it "not land, but cloud."

The three ships set a record: they became the first ones ever, so far as we know, to sail three weeks out of sight of land.

The sailors grew restless. The trade wind usually blew, and, when it did, always blew toward the west; it unnerved them. It pushed the ships to the west so well that the men thought they would never be able to sail back home again. Columbus sailed on and on—due west, always west.

On October 3, Columbus wrote in his journal, they saw vegetation "very fresh and bearing something like fruit." That looked like a sure sign of land.

On October 7 came the second false sighting of land. Men aboard the *Niña* thought they saw it. They didn't.

As October moved along, the men saw birds continually. "A white bird which seemed to be a gull," Columbus said. They saw petrels, boobies, frigate birds. "A great flock of birds," said Columbus, "on October 7 passed from north to southwest." Terns. Ducks. "Many land birds," Columbus noted. At night the men saw birds passing steadily across the moon.

Columbus may have followed the golden plover to land. In autumn it migrates over the seas from North to South America.

At that time, some authorities say, Columbus and his ships, sailing west, were headed for the southern tip of Florida.

Columbus's birds were also seen by the captain of the *Pinta*, Martin Alonso Pinzón. Martin Pinzón believed that the birds knew where they were headed. Pinzón advocated a change in course from west to southwest. Columbus made the change.

On the night of October 10–11, flights of migrating birds overhead, silhouetted against the moon, were apparently a legitimate sign of land ahead—ahead, that is, of the birds.

Columbus followed them.

What birds were they? Macaws or parrots—land birds—were perhaps some of them.

They might also have included lesser golden plovers in their autumn migration from Canada's Upper Hudson's Bay and from Newfoundland and New England all the way to South America. The lesser golden plover, which weighs no more than two or three chicken's eggs, is believed to be capable of flying without stopping for a distance as long as 2400 miles (3800 km). It goes all the way to its winter home on the pampas (plains) of Argentina.

The direction it was flying could well have pointed the way toward land for the three ships, the *Niña*, the *Pinta*, and the *Santa María*.

Chapter Eight

FOLLOWING
A GLEAM

October 11, 1492. Columbus wrote in his journal that his men saw "a green reed near the ship." He also noted another sign of land—and of human beings: "Those on the *Pinta* . . . secured a small stick, carved, as it appeared, with iron, and a piece of cane, and other vegetation, which grows on land, and a small board." The board apparently had been shaped by men with tools.

About ten o'clock that night, Columbus himself, standing atop the castle (the covered cabin) at the *Santa María*'s stern, saw lights ahead, glowing. The lights rose and fell once or twice, "like a wax candle," Columbus said. He thought the lights might indicate nearby land. A sailor, Pedro Gutierrez, also saw the lights in sudden and passing gleams.

Columbus shortened sail and waited.

Columbus, sailing on and on, as he did, into unknown seas, time and again sailed into mysteries. It is still a mystery what those lights were. Some biologists today say that they were made by, of all things, worms—possibly 1-inch-long (2.5-cm) worms of the West Indies and Bermuda that come up to spawn a couple of nights after the full moon, and, as they do, show an ethereal light on the surface of the water.

Or perhaps they were palolo worms, which are segmented, and as long as 16 inches (40 cm). It is not the entire worm that rises to spawn. It is the hind (or rear) parts that, at night, have broken off and floated to the surface, carrying—male or female as the case may be—sperm or eggs. The front parts of the worms stay in burrows in rocks or dead coral in the dark water.

On the surface, the hind parts glow—beautifully, luminously, eerily, iridescently. At sunlight, they writhe around and eject eggs or sperm into the sea. These join, and by sunset, larvae (tiny young ones) are swimming around.

After about three days on the surface, the larvae sink into the depths to enter burrows similar to those their parents lived in.

With no mouths to eat with, the rear halves that have brought up the eggs and sperm die or are themselves eaten. Besides putting on their display in the West Indies, where Columbus was, the palolo worms also swarm at full moon in October in the Pacific Ocean near the Fiji and Samoan islands, where they are food from the sea, eaten by humans.

Never were worms—if they were worms—more important to men than they were that night to Columbus.

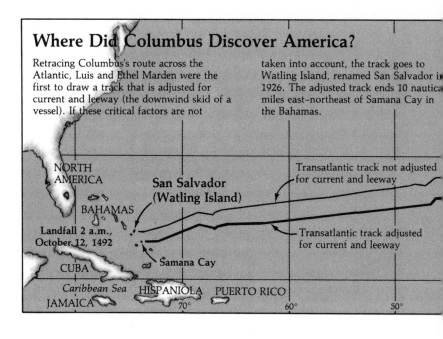

Where Did Columbus Discover America?

Retracing Columbus's route across the Atlantic, Luis and Ethel Marden were the first to draw a track that is adjusted for current and leeway (the downwind skid of a vessel). If these critical factors are not taken into account, the track goes to Watling Island, renamed San Salvador in 1926. The adjusted track ends 10 nautical miles east–northeast of Samana Cay in the Bahamas.

NORTH AMERICA

San Salvador (Watling Island)

Transatlantic track not adjusted for current and leeway

BAHAMAS

Landfall 2 a.m., October 12, 1492

Transatlantic track adjusted for current and leeway

CUBA

Samana Cay

Caribbean Sea   HISPANIOLA   PUERTO RICO

JAMAICA

70°   60°   50°

Columbus crossed the Atlantic to—where?
To the Bahama Islands, but which one?
For the National Geographic Society, Luis and Ethel

Columbus's fate—and the fate of a good many other persons besides—may have been determined by the activities of the palolo worms. There is no way to be sure; this is a mystery that may never be solved.

At 2:00 A.M., a sailor on the *Pinta*, Roderigo de Triano, announced that he saw land. The land was 6 or 8 miles (9.6 or 12.8 km) away.

As other sailors, including the Phoenicians and St. Brendan and the Vikings or Norsemen and the

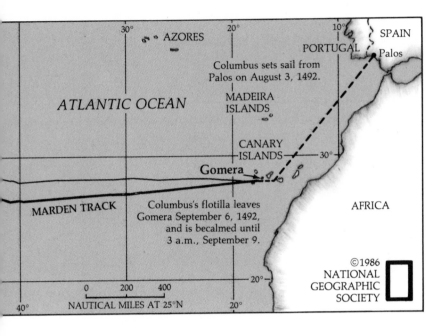

Marden drew a track that led to Samana Cay (or Key). Previously, San Salvador (Watling Island) had been believed to be Columbus's first landing spot.

Portuguese, had come upon islands in unknown oceans, so now did Columbus.

Later that morning, October 12, 1492, thirty-three days—just over a month—after leaving the Canary Islands, Christopher Columbus first set foot in the Western Hemisphere.

He and his people stepped onto one of the Bahama Islands—somewhere in the Atlantic Ocean, approximately 400 miles (640 km) southeast of today's Miami, Florida.

Another of the mysteries Columbus sailed into appears right here: What island was it? Where exactly did he land?

Perhaps because Columbus had altered his course from west to southwest to follow a flock of birds, he had landed in the Bahama Islands of the West Indies instead of on Florida and the continent of North America. Although Spanish explorers later were to reach North America, particularly the Gulf Coast and California, Arizona, and New Mexico, most of North America was left for other Europeans to explore—and to settle. The Spaniards instead would go to Latin America.

"Never did the flight of birds have more important consequences," said a German, Alexander von Humboldt. Humboldt, around 1799–1800—over three hundred years after Columbus had opened the door for the Spaniards—explored Spanish South America.

On the shore of the island he had reached, Columbus raised the flag of Spain's Queen Isabella and King Ferdinand.

His people, Columbus said, "saw many green trees and much water and fruit of various kinds." There were people there: the inhabitants brought "parrots and cotton threads on balls." All of the natives he saw, Columbus said, were young.

Columbus had himself rowed all the way around the island. It was small, 13 miles (20.8 km) by 6 miles (9.6 km). The inhabitants called their island Guana-

*Samana Cay today. The solid line indicates
the probable route of the ships to the point
where they dropped anchor. After going
ashore, Columbus and his men used rowboats
to explore more of the coastline (dashed line).*

hani. Columbus named it San Salvador (Holy Savior).

Which Bahama island was it? At least nine islands have been mentioned as possibilities: Samana Cay, Egg Island, East Caicos, Mayaguana, Plana Cays, Cat, Conception, Grand Turk, and Watling. (In 1926, Watling Island was renamed San Salvador.)

Recent evidence points to Samana Cay as the site of Columbus's first landing. Indeed, on Samana Cay, relics, including shell beads and bits of pottery, of ten former native settlements have been found along with part of an earthen vessel used in Spanish ships to carry olives, olive oil, or water.*

---

*Judge, Joseph. "Where Columbus Found the New World." *National Geographic*, November 1986 (Vol. 170, No. 5) 581.

Chapter Nine

NEW SIGHTS
FOR
ALL HANDS

From their very first landing, everything they saw was brand-new to Columbus and his people. They were in a part of the world completely unknown to Europeans. Columbus's journal makes you think they stared with goggling eyes at everything.

"I saw so many islands," wrote Columbus on October 14, 1492, "that I could not decide to which I should go first."

He went on to discover more of the three thousand Bahama Islands, keys, and rocks that begin in the Atlantic 70 miles (112 km) from Florida and stretch 600 miles (960 km), and that cover an area of ocean slightly larger than Great Britain.

From his first landing place, Columbus reached other islands he called Santa Maria de la Concepcion (for Mary, Mother of Christ); Fernandina (for King Ferdinand); Isabella (for the Queen); and the

Sand or Sandy Islands (today's Ragged Island range) near Cuba.

He discovered two big islands: today's Cuba and Haiti-Dominican Republic (which he called Española or Hispaniola).

Columbus had thought he could reach Asia by sailing west across the Atlantic.

He believed that Cuba, which he reached on October 18, 1492, was either Cipangu (Japan) or the mainland of China. (In 1492, Columbus visited only Cuba's north shore; he did not sail around it and learn it was an island.)

Columbus thought that India was nearby, and, accordingly, he called the inhabitants he met Indians.

He described Cuba as "the most lovely that eyes have ever seen; it is full of good harbors and deep rivers . . . very beautiful mountains." He saw "trees, lovely and green, and different from ours . . . there were many birds and small birds which sang very sweetly."

He marveled to find both pines and palms in Cuba.

The Indians Columbus met had canoes that held one man, he said, and canoes that held up to forty-five men, which they paddled—they had no oars and no sails. In a letter of 1493, after his return, Columbus would increase the number of men he had seen in an Indian canoe: "I have seen one of these canoes

*On October 12, 1492, Columbus first
landed on an island in the Bahamas.
Theodore de Bry's later engraving is fanciful.*

with seventy or eighty men in it, each with his paddle."

The Indians' word *canoa* would become the English word *canoe*.

From the Indians, both on Cuba and on other islands, Columbus obtained knowledge of something that after his trip would be useful at sea. Sailors, until then, had slept wherever they flopped on deck—or below deck—on the softest wooden boards they could find. Columbus's people noticed the Indians' hammocks. (The Indian name *hamaca* gave us our word *hammock*.) Hammocks were soon put aboard ships.

With blankets, in a hammock, a sailor actually had a chance to stay warm and dry. For the first time a sailor could get a good night's sleep on a rolling sea. Hammocks were one of the first assets from the Western Hemisphere.

Besides learning about hammocks, Columbus and his people kept a sharp eye peeled for food or anything else that would help their families or other folks back home. Columbus's seamen brought back word of, or samples of, a number of things: maize—the grain that would become today's basic U.S. crop, corn; pumpkins; large snails—the conches, with their beautiful shells, that grow up to a foot (30 cm) long off the southeast Atlantic coast of today's Florida, and 2 feet (60 cm) long at Padre Island, Texas.

What else did they discover? Cassava bread made from the roots of the cassava, or tapioca, plant.

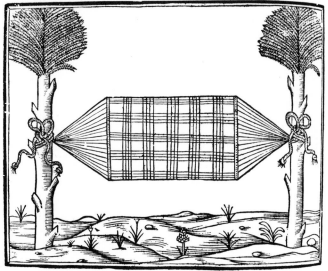

Columbus in 1492 saw Indians in canoes
with paddles (no oars). He saw hammocks.
Sailors at once latched onto hammocks—they
provided a dry place to sleep while at sea.

Tobacco leaves. In Cuba, they saw people with "half-burnt weeds in their hands, being the herbs they are accustomed to smoke." Dyewood. Agave (the Bahamas' century plant). The big lizards eaten in the Caribbean area, known as iguanas. American beans. Wild cotton. Resin from the gumbo-limbo tree. Native creole pepper. The trunkfish. The hutia—an edible Cuban four-legged animal that resembles a large rat. More parrots like some that had been seen on San Salvador, and, presumably, more new species as well.

Columbus saw a tree new to him, growing "even within the sea"—the mangrove—a tree with roots arching high out of the water. At one place, Columbus wrote in his journal, the trees were "so thick a cat couldn't get ashore." Growing on the mangroves were oysters that are today called coon oysters. Columbus theorized falsely that drops of dew falling into their open shells caused pearls to be formed.

Columbus found cassava (manioc) (top left), a tropical food. On the islands he saw parrots (top right), and took some home to Spain. He also came across the up-to-5-foot-long lizard (below), the iguana —used as food in the West Indies and Latin America.

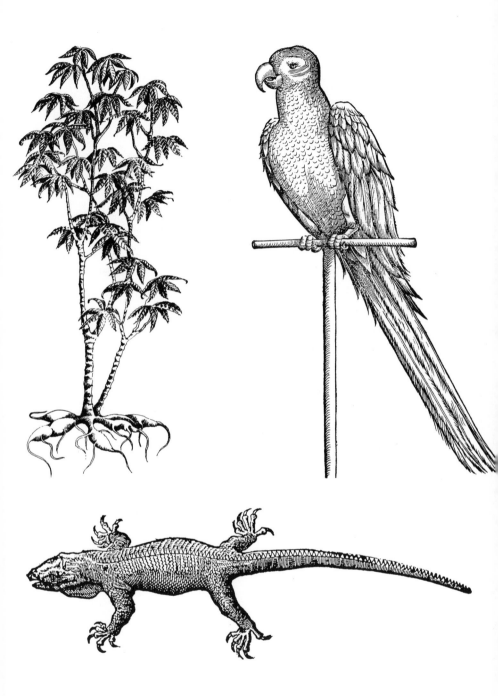

Columbus is said to have found in the West Indies something else: popcorn. The natives were wearing it like corsages.

Columbus also found the sweet potato—and started a long parade. Ocean explorers after him also found the sweet potato, wherever they went: in Central and South America, and also all across the Pacific—on Easter Island and Hawaii, in Polynesia, New Zealand, Indonesia, Malaysia, China, Japan, Africa, and India. Yet the sweet potato may have started in the Americas. Its seeds are killed by salt water, so it could not have floated across the sea. The seed may have been carried from South America across the Pacific by that far traveler that sometimes visits South America on the Pacific side as well as on the Atlantic: the lesser golden plover. The golden plover—the bird whose migration south Columbus may have followed—could have carried the seeds either in its digestive tract or on its feet.

Chapter Ten

MERMAIDS
AND A
LOST COLONY

At Haiti (on the island of Hispaniola), which he reached December 6, 1492, Columbus named a harbor St. Nicholas after a sailor saint whose memory would evolve, over the centuries, into Santa Claus.

Columbus reportedly brought the first hogs to his new discoveries. He is believed to have left eight on Haiti.

Near the mouth of a river, Columbus saw what he thought were three mermaids "which rose well out of the sea—not so beautiful as they are painted."

Some people are convinced that Columbus's mermaids off Haiti were manatees, the big sea mammals related to the African and Asian dugongs. They are frequently seen in West Indian rivers and in Florida.

In Haiti, Columbus heard a bird with a thrushlike song he called a nightingale. It was probably a 10-

inch-long (25-cm) bird with dark gray, light gray, and white feathers that sings both at night and by day, a favorite throughout the U.S. South—a bird that today is living as far north as New York City and Massachusetts: the mockingbird. (There is a rarer Bahama mockingbird.)

On Christmas Day, 1492, the *Santa María*, off Haiti, ran aground and sank. Columbus moved aboard the caravel *Niña*, Little Girl.

From the *Santa María*, timbers were salvaged to build a fort.

About this time, Columbus may have used natural seeps of oil to make the *Niña* and the *Pinta* watertight—an early use of petroleum in the Western Hemisphere.

On January 16, 1493, Columbus, in the *Niña*, sailed for home. He left thirty-nine men under Diego de Arana in Haiti to hold the fort till he returned. After he left, all of them were killed by the Haitians. Thus Columbus's first settlement in the Americas ended in failure.

Columbus would try again.

On the first trip, Columbus reported seeing mermaids. They may have been manatees— fairly common in the West Indies and Florida.

Chapter Eleven

A STORMY
WAY BACK

From Haiti, Columbus sailed north for some distance, then turned east. He now had favorable winds, the westerly anti-trades—blowing from the west— to drive him toward Europe.

On February 3, 1493, Columbus said, he had a difficulty: the north star appeared very high, as at Cape St. Vincent, Portugal, but he "could not take its altitude with the astrolabe or quadrant, as the roll [of the ship] did not permit it."

As Columbus was traveling homeward, a storm battered the *Niña* and separated her from the *Pinta*.

Wrote Columbus in his journal for the night of February 14–15, 1493:

> *All night the Admiral* [Columbus's ship, the Niña] *made flares and the other vessel answered, until, as it seemed, she could do so no more owing to the violence of the storm, and because she was very far out of the course of the Admiral.*

The *Pinta* disappeared—and would not be seen again till she arrived home in Spain.

Columbus was sailing from west to east, the direction in which many storms move in the north Atlantic, and the storm stayed with him. He studied the storms so carefully and accurately that by today's standards he could be classified as an early meteorologist (weather scientist).

His sails were shredded to rags. He himself was in almost as bad shape. He described himself in the third person: "Very crippled in his legs, owing to having been constantly exposed to the cold and water, and owing to the small amount he had eaten."

He was driven to seek shelter anywhere he could find it. He sighted an island. In adverse winds, it took him three days to get there.

He put in at Santa María, the most southern island of the Portuguese Azores, late in February 1493. He did what he could to mend his sails.

He left the Azores and ran into another winter north Atlantic storm. On March 3, 1493, the wind reached hurricane strength "which tore all the sails," Columbus wrote.

On March 4, "in a terrible storm," he scurried for safety—not into a port of Spain, the country that was supporting him, but into the harbor of Spain's competitor, a country that had refused him support: into the mouth of the Tagus River, at Lisbon, Portugal. Here Columbus anchored.

Returning from his first voyage, Columbus, on
March 4, 1493, was driven by a storm into
safe harbor at Lisbon, Portugal (whose king had
refused to back him). Lisbon was then the busiest
port in Europe, and crowded with ships.

Columbus had taken forty-two days to sail from Haiti to Lisbon. His entire round-trip had taken thirty-two weeks.

In the Lisbon harbor was what Columbus described as "the great ship of the King of Portugal." Her master—as a reward for his 1487 trip to discover Africa's Cape of Good Hope—was Bartholomew Diaz. As a representative of King John of Portugal, Diaz soon visited the *Niña* and Columbus.

In return, Columbus paid a courtesy call on the court of Portugal. Speaking to the king, who had refused to back him, Columbus did not minimize his discoveries.

In the employ of the queen, Leonor, there was a new page boy, a boy fresh from an inland mountain region, who was then about thirteen years old. He had chances to stare at Columbus. The lad might have seen the *Niña* in the harbor. He might have seen or heard Columbus around the court. He probably heard talk of Columbus's discoveries, which, because Columbus and others thought they were near India, would be called the West Indies.

The page boy would have heard that Columbus had sailed straight away from the coast, west into the Atlantic, across the Muslims' Green Sea of Darkness.

The boy's name was Fernao de Magelhães e Sousa—in English, Ferdinand Magellan.

Columbus's voyage would influence him for life. Thirty years after he was impressed by Columbus,

After his first voyage, Columbus was asked how
he discovered the New World. He answered
by asking, "How do you stand an egg on end?"
He cracked the bottom of the egg so it stood up.
In other words, it was all in knowing how.

Magellan himself would want to try to sail west across the Atlantic to reach Asia. The result: Magellan did. He would be the first to cross the Atlantic, then to go on across the then-unknown Pacific. He got to the Philippines, and lost his life there. One of his ships, the *Victoria*, would become the first ship ever to sail around the world.

The *Victoria*, under Captain Sebastiano Del Cano, would arrive back in Spain carrying the most valuable cargo her crew could obtain: spices from the Spice Islands, in the East Indies, today Indonesia.

Columbus left Lisbon on March 13, 1493. He sailed south past Cape St. Vincent, where, over sixteen years earlier, a ship carrying him as a seaman had been attacked, and where he had swum ashore.

He reached Palos, Spain, March 15, 1493.

On the same day, by one of those coincidences history cannot explain, Martin Alonso Pinzón and the *Pinta*, separated from Columbus and the *Niña* ever since the storm of February 14–15, also arrived in Palos.

Soon afterward—quite possibly worn out by the voyage—Martin Alonso Pinzón died.

Chapter Twelve

"A NEW WORLD"

At dawn on September 25, 1493, Columbus, now with a title, Admiral of the Ocean Sea, sailed from Cadiz, Spain, to return to the scene of his discoveries. On this his second trip to the Americas, he had the greatest fleet he would ever command: the *Niña* again, thirteen other caravels, and three galleys.

The second voyage was very different from the first. No longer were there three small ships and ninety men alone on an almost-unknown ocean. If nothing else was known, a way across the sea was. Spanish young men no longer were as afraid of the Green Sea of Darkness, the Atlantic, as they had been. Now they volunteered. Some were looking for adventure. Some were looking for spices—then, still long before Magellan, a constant and pressing need. Some were looking for treasure. Many were cheerful—optimistic. Guglielmo Como wrote:

> . . . the last embraces were given by those set-
> ting out on the voyage; the ships (seventeen in-
> stead of three) were hung with tapestry; stream-
> ers were displayed entwined with the ropes; the
> royal standard decorated the stern on all sides.

"They took orange and lemon seeds," the writer Eliza K. B. Dooley noted in her book, *Old San Juan*, "besides fruits and vegetables for planting . . . and horses, cattle, and goats were driven on board. . . ."

The week after Columbus sailed, on October 1, 1493, a young Italian then in Barcelona, Spain, Peter Martyr, wrote a letter to the Archbishop of Brega. The letter told about Columbus's first trip.

"The hidden half of the globe is brought to light," Peter Martyr wrote.

He thought that "hitherto unknown shores will become accessible" and that other sailors would follow Columbus: "For one in emulation of another sets forth on labors and mighty perils."

In another letter a month later, on November 1, 1493, Peter Martyr coined a phrase for what Columbus had found: "A New World."

Some of the sailors on Columbus's second voyage were to emulate him and become known as explorers themselves. One of them, Ponce de Leon, would discover Florida. Another, Antonio de Alaminos, would be one of the discoverers of the Gulf Stream; this is a river in the sea that flows from Florida to

Europe and today aids ships traveling from the United States to Europe.

In October 1493, at sea on his second trip, Columbus and his people were beset by a storm. Then two glowing lights appeared at his masthead. This was St. Elmo's fire, an electrical discharge that appears on ships' masts. It is believed to be a sign of better weather coming, and in this case, it was. The tempest abated. The sea became smooth.

Chapter Thirteen

TO TERRITORY
OF TODAY'S
UNITED STATES

Again Columbus found himself in unknown waters, and again discovered unknown islands. On this second voyage he sailed in a more southerly direction across the Green Sea of Darkness. This time he found twenty large islands and forty small ones.

Among them: the Isle of Pines, near Cuba; the Virgin Islands east of Puerto Rico—St. Croix, St. Thomas, and St. John are today under the American flag; and Antigua, St.-Kitts Nevis, Montserrat, Marie Galante, Guadeloupe, and Jamaica.

Columbus visited only one of the more than a hundred scattered Virgin Islands and keys. He named it Santa Cruz (Holy Cross). It became St. Croix (Americans today pronounce it "Saint Croy"). At St. Croix, Carib Indians in a canoe fired arrows dipped in poisonous sap from the manchineel tree. When their canoe was rammed by one of Columbus's ships, they continued, while swimming, to fire their arrows.

Columbus had a couple of skirmishes
with cannibals. This was a later engraving
—perhaps imaginary.

The Indians, who were cannibals, were commanded by a woman. Researchers have found (as did Columbus) that Carib women were leaders.

They were builders, warriors, gardeners, artisans, and cooks. They thatched palm fronds for the tent-like shelters that served as homes.

They helped build canoes. They made the animal-skin aprons that were the Caribs' only clothing. They raised the crops, fashioned cooking pots from island clay and dishes from hollowed-out calabashes, the hard soccer-ball-shaped fruit of the calabash tree. They twisted and knotted jungle vines into sleeping hammocks and baskets.*

At mealtimes, the Indians turned the jungle-vine baskets upside-down—for tables.

Columbus named the islands the Virgins after a fourth-century English Celtic princess, Ursula, who, with eleven thousand virgins, set out on a pilgrimage to Rome. At prayer, they were massacred. Veils of sea spray rising against the shore are supposed to have reminded Columbus of Ursula and her companions at prayer.

On November 19, 1493, Columbus landed on a large island that is today under the American flag: Puerto Rico.

**The American West Indies,* by Sabra Holbrook. New York: Meredith Press, 1969.

Columbus called the island San Juan Bautista, for Saint John the Baptist. There he found springs of water, and thereafter regarded the island as a supply station for food and water.

The Arawak Indians he encountered there were advanced: they were hunters, fishermen, and carvers of stone. They built houses around a village square. They had an organized system of government. Village chieftains reported to regional chieftains who reported to a top chief of all.

On this trip, Columbus's people found tasty wild pigeons, large oysters, and large conch shells "as large as a calf's head." They ate a barkless dog—perhaps the coati, an animal with a pointed head somewhat like a dog's—and did not like it. They saw what was for Europeans a new bird: the flamingo.

They saw a flock of countless cormorants, a sea dense with turtles, a snowstorm of butterflies, and more of the coon oysters clinging to mangrove roots.

Columbus's sailors also observed what they called "a repulsive sea monster." No one knows what it was.

At Jamaica, he found the inhabitants sailing in canoes up to 90 feet (27 m) long—longer than many of Columbus's ships—and 8 feet (2.4 m) wide. The canoes were made of single trunks of giant mahogany trees.

At one point, Columbus's people ran into a sea full of black volcanic sand. This brought back grim and

On his second trip to the New World, Columbus saw many cormorants (left), and his men were the first Europeans to see the flamingo (right).

On his second voyage, Columbus found oysters (top), some growing on the roots of mangrove trees. He came upon a food Europeans never had imagined—the pine-apple (this drawing from a 1547 account of the West Indies by Oviedo).

foreboding memories of names that for centuries people had called the almost-unknown Atlantic Ocean: the Dark Sea (according to the Romans) and the Green Sea of Darkness (by the Muslims).

On Guadeloupe, Columbus's shore parties found cotton cloth, hammocks (again), pottery, domesticated mallard ducks, tame parrots, and sweet potatoes (again), and—entirely unknown to Europeans—pineapples.

Columbus ran into another mystery: his people came upon what appeared to be a timber from a European ship, and an iron pot apparently from a European ship. Could others have been there ahead of them? This mystery will probably never be cleared up.

Chapter Fourteen

TURTLE SOUP, LONGHORN CATTLE

Near Cuba, Columbus learned a way a person might obtain food for his family. At a group of small islands south of Cuba, Jardin de la Reina, the Garden of the Queen (Columbus's name), the inhabitants fished by capturing remoras, or shark suckers. These are the fish with flat suckers on their heads with which they grip on to sharks and obtain free rides—and hang on to other kinds of large sea animals as well. A rope was tied around the tail of a captured remora. The remora was dropped into the sea at the end of the rope. The remora would fasten its sucker on to a fish or even on to a great sea turtle. The line could be hauled in, the grip would not let go, and the fish or turtle would be caught.

Right here Europeans learned about the green turtle. Without its fresh meat, according to some authorities, the European exploration of the New World from the 1500s to the 1900s would not have been possible. The turtle was to be a food supply for

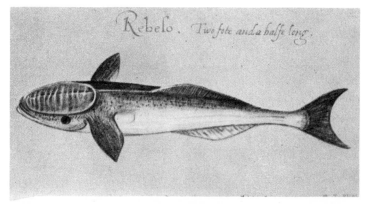

Columbus's people saw natives using a fish, the remora, with a sucker on its flat head to hang onto large sea animals such as the green turtle, to obtain food.

countless sailors. It meant food to Europeans back home as well: turtle soup.*

The Indians Columbus saw caught young remoras, kept and fed them in saltwater, and talked to them to encourage them to catch fish. They were domesticating the remora. This was not the Europeans' discovery of the remora; it had been shown on ancient Greek vases. What *was* significant, though, was that this was one of people's first attempts to domesticate a sea animal. Earlier, Asians and Europeans had raised a fish: carp. Today there is a lot of discussion as to which sea animals might be domesticated, and work is being done on shrimp, fish (trout from the sea and salmon), and shellfish.

On this second voyage, after sunset on November 17, 1493, Columbus reached Haiti, on the island of Hispaniola, at the site where he had left thirty-nine men. Here some of the optimism of the trip turned to grief.

He lit flares. No reply. He fired a cannon. No answering shot.

He landed and found that the settlement he had established had been wiped out.

Wherever they went, the Spaniards (and other sailors, until the 1800s), carried cattle in their ships to provide milk and fresh meat. In those days of no refrigeration, there was no other way to have fresh

*American Museum of Natural History, October 20, 1977.

food. For the same reason, the sailing ships carried sheep, goats, hens, geese, ducks, and hogs. They often also carried horses.

Whenever they landed on an unknown island or shore, the Spaniards turned some of the animals loose—in the hope that they would survive and breed and multiply and that any later Spanish sailors would find them and be helped by the animals.

On this second trip, Columbus brought to Haiti the biggest four-footed animals that Haitians had seen: horses and longhorn cattle. The Spaniards in time would carry horses and cattle farther: to Mexico, Texas, Florida, and other Spanish discoveries or colonies in the region.

Almost four hundred years afterward, the U.S. Civil War disrupted agriculture, and Americans needed all the food they could get. Starting in 1866, just after the war, the wild descendants of the longhorns were rounded up in Texas and driven north, by the cowboys, to help feed Americans.

Many of the horses the cowboys rode were descendants of Spanish horses that, like the longhorns, had run wild. So are some of the wild horses that still roam free in the American West.

In 1494, on a rocky islet south of Hispaniola, Columbus's men killed eight "sea wolves"—probably the first record of the West Indies monk seal. The monk seal is rare now, living somewhere among the countless lonesome West Indies rocks and islets (cays, or keys).

On this second voyage, Columbus brought sugarcane to Haiti and to the New World.

Quickly thereafter, cane fields spread throughout the Caribbean. A Spaniard after Columbus, Hernán Cortés, would take cane to Mexico. Another, Francisco Pizarro, would take cane to Peru.

By the year 1600, raw sugar production in tropical America, that is, in Central and South America and the Caribbean islands, was to be the largest industry—in the world.

Twelve of Columbus's ships headed home on February 2, 1494. Columbus lingered on. A caravel, the *India*, was built from scratch as he stayed. That sailors so far from home could build a vessel is surprising. This will give you an idea how competent they were.

With two caravels, the *India* and the *Niña*, Columbus started home on March 10, 1496.

As well as taking new food home to Europe, Columbus brought new food to the New World. On his second voyage, he took sugarcane to Haiti. By 1600, sugarcane in the New World was the largest industry on earth.

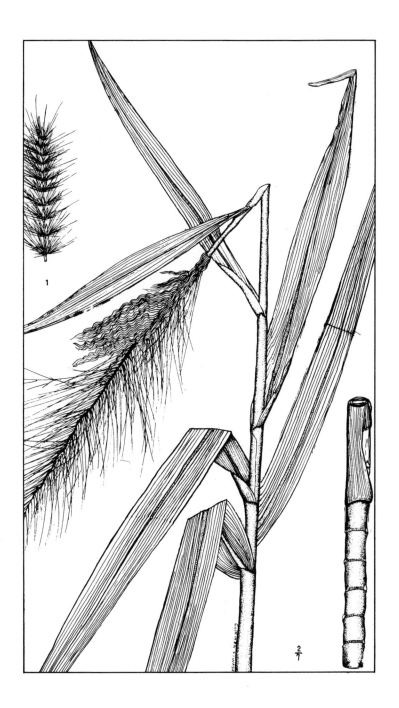

1

2
⁄
7

Columbus had two hundred of his people, some sick, and thirty Indians, crammed into the two little vessels which would have been crowded with a total of fifty sailors for them both. Few of the Indians survived the voyage.

Head winds made it a long, slow trip.

On June 7, 1496, Columbus, with the instinct or knowledge of a born seaman, announced they were off Portugal. Next day they saw the coast.

Three days later, flags and pennants flying, the two ships entered the harbor of Cadiz, Spain.

Chapter Fifteen

TWO OTHER
SAILORS

Spain was not the only European power eager to find a western route to the riches of the East. There was competition from Britain and Portugal.

After Diaz of Portugal had passed Africa's Cape of Good Hope in 1487, and after Columbus's first two voyages for Spain, Britain's King Henry VII sent out, from Bristol, England, an Italian: John Cabot. As had Columbus, Cabot had been born in Genoa, Italy.

In 1497, Cabot—with a crew of eighteen men in the 50-ton ship *Mathew,* or *Matthew*—tried to find a northwest passage to India and Asia and spices. Seven weeks out he landed where many believe the Norseman Leif Ericsson had been in A.D. 1000. Henry VII named Cabot's landing place "a new Founde land": Newfoundland.

At sea the crew caught plenty of fish: they were near the fertile fishing grounds of the Grand Banks.

Cabot's trip gave Britain a basis for claims to North America.

What with Spain and Portugal cutting off the possible southern routes to Asia, Britain would for hundreds of years seek the northwest passage. Today, occasionally, ships cross the world above Canada. But there is no satisfactory route.

The year after Columbus returned from his second trip to the New World, another man made a voyage toward India. He sailed under the flag of Portugal, and he sailed east around Africa—instead of west as had Columbus. His name was Vasco da Gama.

In 1497, Da Gama, with four ships, left Portugal. He followed Bartholomew Diaz's 1487 route around the southern tip of Africa. Diaz had supervised the building of Da Gama's ships and had sailed with him part way.

Then, after rounding the southern end of Africa, Da Gama reached Malindi (in Kenya) where he picked up a Muslim pilot, Ibn Majid. Ibn Majid got Da Gama across from the east African coast to India.

On May 22, 1498, ten and a half months out of Portugal, Da Gama reached the western, or Malabar, coast of India. Da Gama had found his route to Asia, where Columbus and Cabot had not.

The way east to India and Asia and spices was established—and Da Gama's route soon would be busy with ships.

Chapter Sixteen

A NEW
CONTINENT

On May 30, 1498, Columbus, with eight ships, departed San Lucar, on the Guadalquivir River, Spain, to make his third trip to what Peter Martyr had called his New World. Only a few days earlier, Vasco da Gama had reached India.

One of Columbus's ships again was the *Niña*. Since his second voyage, the *Niña* had survived a hurricane and capture by pirates.

Again Columbus sailed into unknown or almost-unknown seas. He went far south of his previous routes and encountered tropical conditions.

This time Columbus stopped at the Madeira Islands, the Canaries, and the Cape Verde Islands. Between 10 degrees north and the equator, he ran into furnace heat and windless days. He was in the doldrums. He was becalmed and drifting for eleven days altogether. Then the trade winds picked up.

On July 31, in the Caribbean Sea, when one ship had a single cask of water remaining, he watched as three lush green hills rose over the horizon. They all belonged to one island. He had placed this voyage under the protection of the Holy Trinity, and he named the island Trinidad.

He sailed between Trinidad, and, to the south of it, a continent that had been entirely unknown, South America.

A writer of plays, Seneca, in Rome thirteen hundred years earlier, had predicted that there would be discovered a vast new land west across the Atlantic Ocean.

I don't know what Seneca based his prediction on. But six hundred years before Christ, Phoenician sailors, from the eastern Mediterranean, are believed to have sailed around Africa—and just might have been blown to Brazil. A fragmentary record suggests it. Seneca might have known of the Phoenicians.

In 1498, Columbus was about to prove Seneca's prophecy.

Between Trinidad and the Cape of Paria, today's Venezuela, South America, there was a turbulent current. Columbus called the place the Mouth of the Dragon.

On August 5, 1498, for the first time, Columbus reached the mainland. Shortly afterward, when he noticed the great volume of fresh water the Orinoco River pours into the sea, he thought the land might be a continent—and not another island.

North of the Venezuelan coast, he found more islands: Grenada, Tobago, and Margarita.

Columbus's crew on this trip observed West Indian cedars, cabbage palms, mountains "covered with monkeys," mahogany, more mangrove trees with tiny coon oysters in their roots (which Columbus had seen in 1492 and 1493), and pearl fisheries.

The pearl fisheries were in the Gulf of Paria, in the lower Caribbean, and at Margarita and nearby islands. Around the necks of the Indian women were splendid pearls—to which they attached small value. The Spaniards and Indians later quarreled over the pearls, a fight resulted, and some Spaniards were eaten by the Indians.

Columbus had found the only places in the Atlantic where pearls were gathered.

From the island of Margarita, Columbus shaped a course for Hispaniola (Haiti-Dominican Republic).

He was in an unknown sea. All the lands he had seen since the Cape Verde Islands he himself had discovered. He had not met one other ship. And yet his course to Hispaniola was direct—the best possible.

On August 31, 1498, he anchored in today's Dominican Republic.

Later historians were to remark on Columbus's great navigational skills. His biographer, Samuel Eliot Morison, said, "How he did it, I cannot explain." Said Ernle Bradford, in referring to the course from

On his third voyage, Columbus found today's Venezuela—South America—his only discovery of a continent. On nearby Margarita Island, he found natives diving for pearls.

Margarita to Hispaniola, "The astonishing thing about Columbus is his almost uncanny skill as a dead-reckoning navigator." He added, "The only thing that any sailor would say of him is that he deserves to be called a seaman—and in capital letters."

In 1496 in Hispaniola, between Columbus's second and third voyages, his brother Bartholomew had founded Santo Domingo. That was 111 years before the English reached Virginia to establish the United States. Today, Santo Domingo is the oldest contin-uously occupied city in the Americas.

When Columbus reached Hispaniola, he ran into trouble he could not handle.

At Hispaniola, charges against Columbus boiled up. Among other things, disgruntled Spaniards ac-cused him of being a poor governor of lands he dis-covered. The charges were not unfounded; most of his time was spent at sea.

The criticism had begun long before. In Spain, his enemies had undermined his reputation at court. The Spanish court sent someone out to investigate, a man named Francisco de Bobadilla.

Columbus, in 1500, eight years after he had first sailed to San Salvador in the West Indies, was sent back to Cadiz, Spain, in chains. After he arrived, Queen Isabella had him released. But never would Columbus entirely regain favor.

Chapter Seventeen

LAST TRIP

In 1499–1500, a sailor who had been along on Columbus's second voyage, Alonso de Ojeda (Hojeda or Ojera), heard of Columbus's Gulf of Paria, and the pearls there, and went after them. Ojeda found villages astride waterways; the name Venezuela, "little Venice," was born.

With Ojeda was a man from Florence, Italy, who was then living in Seville, Spain: Amerigo Vespucci.

In January or February 1500, Vicente Yáñez Pinzón, Columbus's captain of the *Niña* in 1492, was exploring the northeast coast of what is now Brazil. He saw a broad, yellow flood foaming out to sea. He followed it and—exactly on the equator—he discovered one of the globe's great geographical features: the 135-mile-wide (217-km) mouth of the Amazon River. Then Pinzón sailed north and west all the way to Costa Rica, Central America.

Pinzón's ship may have been Columbus's *Niña*.

Shortly afterward in 1500, Pedro Alvares Cabral of Portugal, with Bartholomew Diaz along, took possession of Brazil for Portugal. Heading up a second Portuguese expedition to India (after Vasco da Gama in 1497), Cabral and Diaz attempted to go east around Africa's Cape of Good Hope. Cabral and four ships made it. Diaz and nine ships were sunk. For Diaz, the Cape of Good Hope was what he had originally named it: the Cape of Storms.

Also in 1500, a Spaniard, Roderigo de Bastidas, an amateur explorer fired up by Columbus's voyages, outfitted a fleet. He hired Juan de la Cosa to pilot it. Bastidas and Cosa tried to steer for South America where they hoped to find a strait across it. Instead, they came upon a new land that would be called New Spain, today Mexico.

Starting from Cadiz, Spain, May 9, 1502, Columbus, about fifty years old, encountered favorable winds that took his four caravels across the Atlantic in twenty-one days, on his fourth and last—and fastest—voyage. He named it the High Voyage.

His largest caravel was 70 tons.

He reached the island today called Martinique. He anchored at St. Lucia, like Martinique one of today's Windward Islands in the West Indies. That was probably the discovery of the island.

The next stop was the island of Hispaniola.

Francisco de Bobadilla, the man who had investigated Columbus and had him returned from his third voyage, shackled, to Spain, was himself about to return to Spain. Columbus, sensing an approaching hurricane, warned Bobadilla's fleet not to sail. It did. Bobadilla, along with many others, was drowned.

Columbus had found a place to anchor in the lee of the land. "The storm was terrible," Columbus later wrote to Ferdinand and Isabella. "During that night it badly damaged my ships, dragging them all away so that each feared that the others were lost." Nevertheless, Columbus and his vessels weathered the storm.

Columbus, still hoping to find Asia or Japan, again sailed west—farther west than ever—and again he entered almost-unknown seas.

He got to Honduras in Central America. On islands off Honduras, the Indians used a nut—cacao—as money. It was to become a new drink for Europeans and Americans: cocoa.

Following the coast southeast, he looked for a strait to take him through. He coasted along today's Nicaragua, Costa Rica, and Panama.

He suffered hardships: storms, rain that lasted six weeks. "Terrible," said Columbus, "with never-ending rain, thunder, and lightning."

When conditions were better, on September 14, 1502, he found a cape he named Gracias á Dios ("Thanks to God"). Probably off Nicaragua, at a river's mouth, a boat overturned, drowning all the sail-

During his third voyage, Columbus was accused
of being a bad colonial governor. Francisco de
Bobadilla sent him home in chains. On his fourth
trip, Columbus warned Bobadilla not to sail
himself—a hurricane was approaching. Bobadilla
left anyway—and was never seen again.

ors in the boat. Columbus called the stream the River of the Disaster.

In December 1502, the weather got worse again: torrential rain, thunder, lightning. On a frightening night, December 13, Columbus saw water that whirled up to a pyramid, with a cloud, or inverted cone, coming down to meet it: a waterspout.

Other conditions got worse, too. Sails were frayed. The men were sick and worn out. Food almost ran out. There was weevily biscuit—the crews ate it after dark so as not to see the weevils. They ate sharks as well.

Columbus found low islands covered with turtles and accordingly named them Las Tortugas. This time his men saw large schools of sharks. They captured a manatee, and, presumably, learned not to mistake it for a beautiful mermaid. They harpooned one of the great flat fish of the open sea, a giant manta ray. They probably saw alligators (later Spanish explorers would see them in Florida) and a spider monkey.

Diego Mendez, along on this last voyage of Columbus, said that the teredo, or shipworm, bored into the hulls of the ships until all the bailing and pumping of water that the crew could do would not keep out the sea. The great teredo worm of the tropics grows up to several feet long and as thick as a person's arm.

At Jamaica, which he had discovered on his second trip, Columbus ran his worm-riddled ships onto a beach and made the hulls into houses. He sent Diego Mendez, with seven others, to Hispaniola for help. In a native canoe rigged with a sail, they set out across 108 miles (173 km) of ocean. Mendez failed, and returned.

Mendez made a second try. This time he had with him another citizen (like Columbus) of Genoa, Bartolomeo Fieschi. There were two boats, both native canoes. Each canoe held six Europeans and ten Indians.

Mendez, Fieschi, and their company did reach Hispaniola, but Columbus had no way of knowing it. No one would volunteer to sail back and tell him.

For Columbus, waiting on Jamaica, months and months crept by.

The Jamaican natives refused to provide enough food. Columbus was desperate. He knew an eclipse of the moon was due on February 29, 1504. He predicted it. It came, and he pretended to end it. The natives became more cooperative.

Mendez, at Santo Domingo, on the island of Hispaniola, encountered eight months of bureaucratic delays. He eventually bought a ship that had arrived from Spain.

Mendez said he "loaded her with provisions, with bread and wine and flesh and pigs and sheep and fruites, and sent her to where the Admiral was."

The caravel reached Jamaica on June 28, 1504. Columbus had been marooned there for one year and five days.

On his fourth and last voyage,
Columbus was mistreated
by the natives. He knew
an eclipse of the moon was
coming, and predicted it
and pretended to end it.
They were awed.

Chapter Eighteen

THE LAST
VOYAGE HOME

Columbus on his fourth and last trip found more new food: red and white beans; a kind of wild turkey; and wine made from maize, palm, and pineapples.

Other foods were found by the Spaniards in the Americas: the avocado in Mexico; beans—lima beans, kidney beans, string beans, shell beans, pea beans; the papaya, with its yellow fruit; the tomato, long thought poisonous, but eventually accepted as food; and the potato—in Chile, Peru, Ecuador, Colombia, and elsewhere.

It has been said that the most important gift the New World gave to Europe was not treasure, but a great variety of food.*

*Roy Chapman Andrews, *This Amazing Planet* (New York: G. P. Putnam's Sons, 1937) p. 117. See also the American Museum of Natural History's magazine *Natural History* (August 1987), p. 66.

Spanish and other European sailors also introduced new foods into the lands they found.

Citrus fruits—oranges, lemons, limes, etc.—which are the most important tropical and subtropical fruits, were brought by the Spanish and Portuguese to the West Indies and from there went to North and South America.

The mango was taken by the Portuguese from tropical east Asia to Brazil.

Into the West Indies, the sailors and explorers introduced bamboo, mangoes, bananas, and the coconut palm (from Panama).

All of these foods are today thought of as native to the West Indies. They are not.

On September 12, 1504, in the caravel that had picked him up in Jamaica, Columbus sailed from Santo Domingo for Spain. From her deck, he looked back at Hispaniola and his New World for the last time.

Columbus, ill, had a rough crossing. On November 7, 1504, he landed at San Lucar. The trip had taken fifty-six days.

On November 26, 1504, Columbus's friend, Queen Isabella, died.

A year and a half later, on May 10, 1506, Columbus, fifty-four years of age and out of favor at the Spanish court, also died. At his bedside in Valladolid, Spain, were his sons Diego and Fernando (Ferdinand), and his younger brother, Diego. Bar-

The coconut palm—today a symbol of the West Indies—was actually found by the Spanish on the Pacific coast of Panama. They spread it around.

tholomew was away. Also present were Bartolomeo Fieschi from Genoa and Captain Diego Mendez. They were the men who had sailed across an open ocean, in canoes, from Jamaica to Santo Domingo to obtain help for the stranded Columbus.

Mendez had been thanked. "As Columbus told me later in Spain," Mendez wrote, "he had never in his life known so joyful a day, for he had never expected to leave that place alive."

Columbus never had stopped believing that he had reached the vicinity of Asia. According to one modern assessment, "History fails to record another case than Columbus's of such momentous success based upon such monumental error."*

In 1507, a monk of St. Die in Lorraine, France, Martin Waldseemüller, made a map that showed some of the new discoveries. He included the continent of South America. He called it America—the earliest use of the name.

It was also the first time the name was set in type, and the first time the name was printed.

That was in honor of a contemporary of Columbus, Amerigo Vespucci. Vespucci, from Florence, Italy, had, around 1500, sailed to South America and far down its Atlantic coast. He himself described four voyages: one private; one under a Spaniard, Alonso

---

*Paul E. Wylie, *Griffith Observatory* magazine, June 1962.

de Ojeda; and two for Portugal. His trips appear to have been later than Columbus's first two voyages.

Vespucci was regarded as exceptionally able at figuring precisely where his ship was. On August 6, 1508, he was appointed pilot major—that is, chief pilot—for Spain.

Waldseemüller's name, America, would stick.

Chapter Nineteen

A WORLD
REMEMBERS

Columbus died in obscurity. His New World was named for someone else. His great success would not be clear for years.

But it was a success—one of the greatest for any individual in history. After Columbus, the world changed. The discoveries of one single individual, Columbus, resulted not only in his New World, but in an entire new era. He opened the Age of Exploration, one of the great ages in history—a golden age. There had never been anything like it before.

Columbus was to set in motion the greatest migrations ever, before or since, as European families spread out over the entire globe. As a result of Columbus, millions of men and women, boys and girls, would open new lands, find new food, build new homes across the sea, and improve living everywhere.

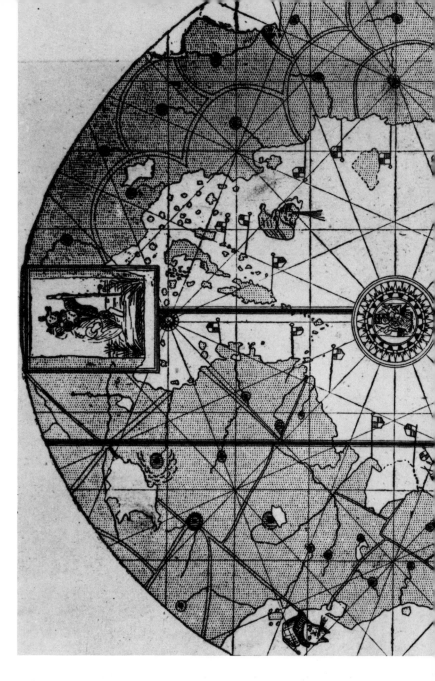

Juan de la Cosa, who sailed with Columbus, may have made this map. It shows (left), Columbus's patron saint, St. Christopher, carrying Christ.

The map crudely shows what may be South America
(facing left, with flags). *Mare Oceanum (center)*
meant Ocean Sea—another name for the Atlantic.

And Columbus began travel around the world—which continues today. There was no worldwide travel before Columbus. Today you can go anywhere. A jet plane is far faster than Columbus's *Niña*, *Pinta*, and *Santa María*. But those three little ships, with the bobbing lanterns at their sterns, showed the way—beyond the horizon and across the sea.

No European before him had known of the Americas. On his second trip, he had stepped ashore on South America. On his last trip, he had reached Central America. He had found dozens of Western Hemisphere islands. His immediate successors would reach North America and the Pacific.

He had made four round-trips to and from the New World—this meant four safe returns across an almost-unknown ocean, the Atlantic. This meant more safety aboard ship for passengers, as the settlers followed Columbus.

Never again would the Atlantic, the Romans' Dark Sea, the Muslims' Green Sea of Darkness, be as terrifying as it had been before him.

During the Age of Exploration set in motion by Columbus—the one hundred and twenty years that followed his death—European sailors reached all the seas and lands on the globe except Antarctica.

The Spanish led the way in the discovery and exploration of new lands:
Florida (1513, Ponce de León)
Pacific Ocean (1513, Vasco Núñez de Balboa)

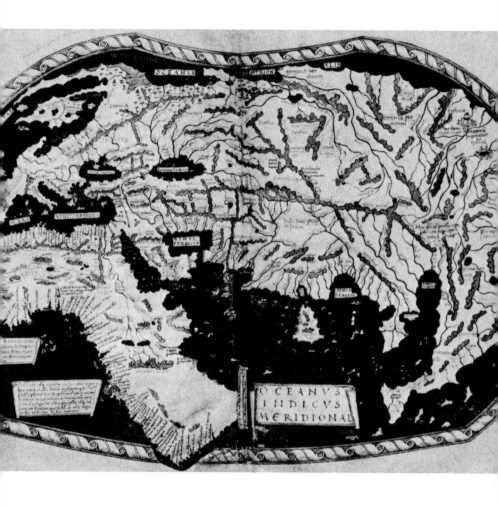

A map of 1492 shows the known world before Columbus's first trip. It did not show the size of the Atlantic (at left), North America, Central America, and South America (all unknown), Australia (unknown), or the islands of Japan off Asia (right). All were discovered in the Age of Exploration set off by Columbus.

Bermuda (1515, Juan de Bermudez)

Texas (1519, Alonso de Pineda)

Philippine Islands and first circumnavigation of world (1519–21, Ferdinand Magellan and Juan Sebastián de Elcano)

Mexico (1519, Hernando Cortés)

Florida, Georgia, North and South Carolina, and maybe Virginia (1521, Francisco Gordillo and Pedro de Quexos)

South Carolina (1526, Luis Vasquez de Ayllon)

West coast of South America (1526, Francisco Pizarro)

Florida, Alabama, Mississippi, and maybe Galveston, Texas (1528, Panfilo de Narvaez and Cabeza de Vaca. They were the first Europeans to see buffalo.)

Peru (1531, Francisco Pizarro)

Plymouth, Massachusetts (1534–35, Esteban Gomez— eighty-five years before the Pilgrims)

Lower California (1536, Hernando Cortés)

New Mexico and Arizona (1539, Francisco Marcos de Niza)

South and North Carolina, Alabama, Arkansas and its hot springs, Oklahoma, Tennessee at today's Memphis, and the Mississippi River (1539– 42, Hernando de Soto.)

Arizona, New Mexico, Oklahoma, Kansas, Texas and its Palo Duro Canyon, and perhaps Colorado and Nebraska (1540–42, Francisco Vasques de Coronado. His companion Garcia Lopez de Cardenas was the first European to see the Grand Canyon.)

California and the bays of Monterey and San Diego
(1542, Juan Rodriguez Cabrillo)
Oregon (1542, Bartholomew Ferraro)
Hawaii, maybe (1555, Juan Gaetano)
St. Augustine, Florida, oldest continuously inhab-
ited city in the U.S. (1565, Pedro Menendez)
Pacific Ocean islands (1606, Pedro Fernandez de
Queiros)

The Spanish continued exploring North America until
the time of the American Revolution. In January
1774—four years ahead of Britain's James Cook—Juan
Perez got to Nootka Sound and Vancouver Island in
today's western Canada. In 1769, the Spanish found
an island in San Francisco Bay—Alcatraz. In 1781,
they established Los Angeles.

Sailors of other nations joined to discover almost the
whole world—the world you know today—during
the Age of Exploration.

Australia, maybe (1503, Paulair de Gonneville for
Portugal)
Spice Islands in the East Indies (early 1500s, the Por-
tuguese)
Indonesia (1511, Portugal's Antonio de Abreu sailed
from the Indian Ocean into the Pacific)
Coast of North America—North Carolina, Mary-
land, Virginia, Delaware, New Jersey, New York
harbor, Long Island, Rhode Island, and maybe
Plymouth, Massachusetts (1524, Giovanni da
Verrazano, an Italian sailing for France)

Canada, the St. Lawrence River, and the site of Montreal (1534, 1535–36, and 1541–42, Jacques Cartier)

Japan (1542, three Portuguese, blown there by mistake by a storm)

Around the world (1577–80, Francis Drake for England)

Around the world (1585–7, Thomas Cavendish for England)

North Carolina, where colony failed (1584–87, Walter Raleigh for England)

In the early part of the seventeenth century, Europeans continued to cross the Atlantic to explore—and sometimes settle—new lands:

Quebec, Maine, Great Lakes, Martha's Vineyard, and Lake Champlain (1603–09, Samuel de Champlain for France)

Australia (1605, William Janszoon for Holland)

Jamestown, Virginia (1607, John Smith established the first British colony in North America.)

New York (1609, Henry Hudson)

Bermuda (1609, George Somers established the second British colony in the New World)

New York (1610, Adriaen Block for Holland)

Plymouth, Massachusetts (1620, the second British colony on the North American continent)

Manhattan Island (1626, the Dutch, for trinkets worth about twenty-four dollars, bought what is today's New York City from the Canarsie Indians)

"The whole history of the Americas," said Samuel Eliot Morison, "stems from the four voyages of Columbus."*

Snubbed, shoved aside, and neglected when he died, Columbus was to be posthumously showered with recognition. Over the last five hundred years, as the world has realized what his four voyages meant, Columbus has received one accolade after another.

At a house in Valladolid, Spain, a tablet is inscribed: "Here died Columbus." Statues of him are on the beach in Barcelona, Spain, and in Panama. Two towns in Panama are named for him: Cristobal (Christopher) and Colon (Columbus). An entire country in South America is named for him: Colombia. So are Ecuador's Galapagos Islands in the Pacific—they are officially called the Columbus archipelago. Columbus never saw Ecuador, the Galapagos, or even the Pacific.

Colombo (Columbus) is the main seaport on the island of Sri Lanka (formerly Ceylon) in the Indian Ocean. Columbus never saw Sri Lanka or the Indian Ocean either.

There are portraits of Columbus in Genoa, Madrid, Paris, and elsewhere, perhaps as many as eighty altogether. There are models thought to be of the *Niña,* the *Pinta,* and the *Santa María* in a dozen or more museums. In the United States, statues, busts, and paintings of Columbus are in the Capitol and in the Library of Congress at Washington; at the Naval

*From *Admiral of the Ocean Sea* (Boston, Little, Brown, 1940).

Academy in Annapolis; at the Mariners' Museum in Newport News, Virginia; at New York City's Metropolitan Museum of Art; and at Notre Dame University, South Bend, Indiana.

Fifteen U.S. cities are named Columbus. The largest is Columbus, Ohio; population 586,179. The smallest is Columbus, Illinois; population 92. The others are in North Dakota, Montana, New Mexico, Texas, Mississippi, Georgia, North Carolina, Indiana, Wisconsin, Iowa, Nebraska, Kansas, Kentucky. Columbus Day in October is a U.S. federal holiday—with parades.

Today, Christopher Columbus is honored by probably more monuments and place names than any other person in history.

Bibliography

Americas. "Epic of a New World." Supplement on Columbus, vol. 23, no. 10 (October 1971).

Bradford, Ernle. *Christopher Columbus.* New York: Viking Press, 1973.

Columbus, Christopher. *The Journals.* Translated by Cecil Jane. New York: Clarkson N. Potter, 1960.

Deacon, C. E. R., ed. *Seas, Maps and Men.* Garden City, N.Y.: Doubleday, 1962.

Humble, Richard, and the editors of Time-Life Books. *The Explorers.* Alexandria, Va.: Time-Life Books, 1978.

Irving, Washington. *The Life and Voyages of Christopher Columbus.* Chicago: North American Publishing, 1892.

Judge, Joseph. "Where Columbus Found the New World." *National Geographic* 170, no. 5 (November 1986): 567.

Kemp, Peter, ed. *The Oxford Companion to Ships and the Sea.* New York: Oxford University Press, 1976.

Lamb, Harold. *New Found World*. Garden City, N.Y.: Doubleday, 1955.

Lündstrum, Björn. *Columbus*. New York: Macmillan, 1966.

Marden, Luis. "The First Landfall of Columbus." *National Geographic* 170, no. 5 (November 1986): 572–577.

Martínez-Hidalgo, José María. *Columbus' Ships*. Barre, Mass.: Barre Publishers, 1966.

Morison, Samuel Eliot. *Admiral of the Ocean Sea*. Boston: Little, Brown, 1940.

———. *Christopher Columbus, Mariner*. Boston: Little, Brown, 1942.

Olson, Julius E., and Bourne, Edward Baylor, eds. *The Northmen, Columbus and Cabot: A.D. 985–1503*. New York: Barnes & Noble, 1906.

Thacher, John Boyd. *Christopher Columbus: His Life, His Work, His Remains*. 3 vols. New York: G. P. Putnam's Sons, 1903.

Index